BLACK IS BEAUTY

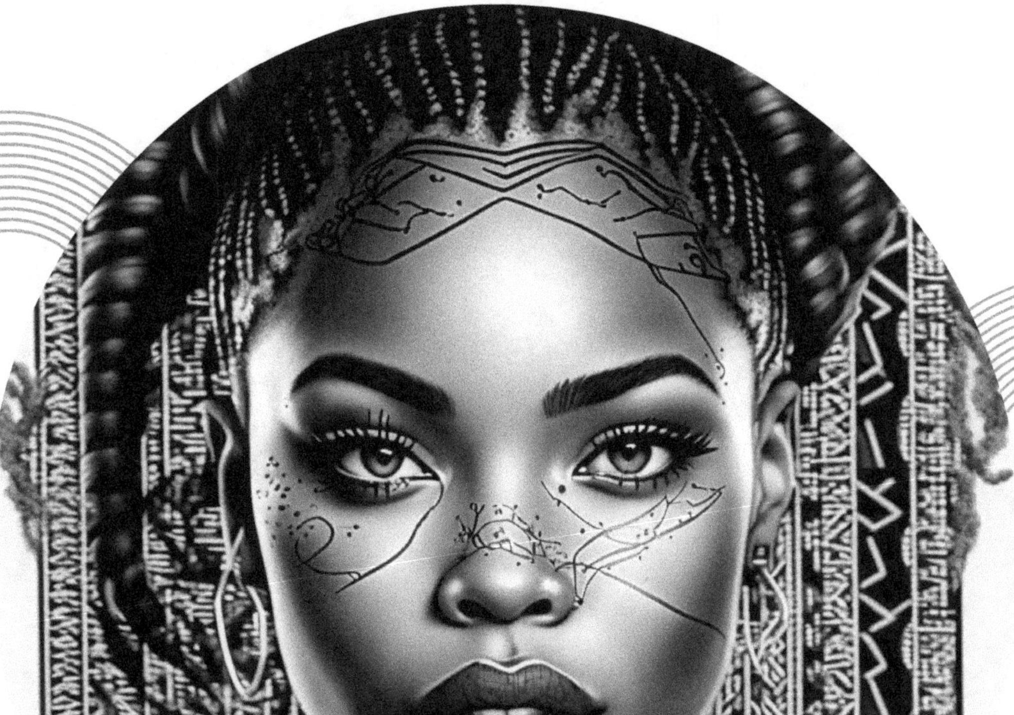

A Coloring Book

BY: DEE HAYES

Dedication

My dearest and most magnificent black women, this dedication is a love letter to you. It's for the ones who have been made to feel inadequate, told that they're too dark or too light, and made to feel ashamed of their natural hair texture. To those who have been told that they don't measure up to some arbitrary standard of beauty, I want you to know that you are more than enough just as you are.

Your beauty is not defined by someone else's narrow definition of what is acceptable. Your strength, resilience, and unbreakable spirit are a testament to the power of the black woman. Your melanin-rich skin is a thing of absolute beauty, and your natural hair texture is a symbol of your strength and individuality.

So to every beautiful black woman out there who has ever been made to feel less than, I dedicate this message to you. Stand tall, embrace your uniqueness, and never forget that you are enough and so much more. You are a force to be reckoned with, and the world is a better place because of you.

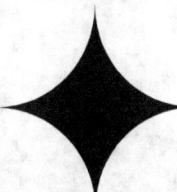

Be comfortable in your black skin. If someone finds a threat in it, then they should visit their psychologist.

———

MITTA XININDLU

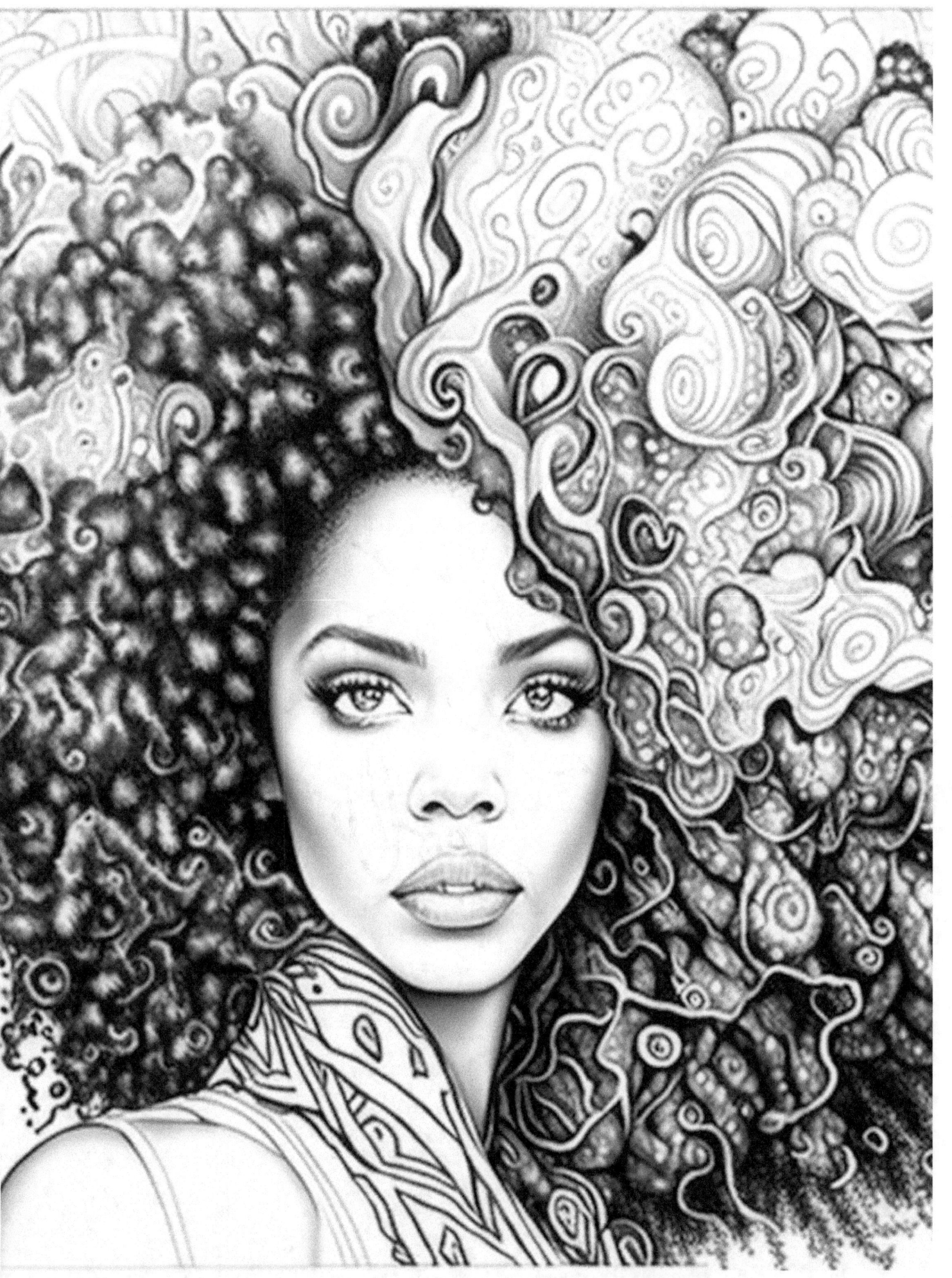

I am dripping melanin and Honey. I am black without apology

♡

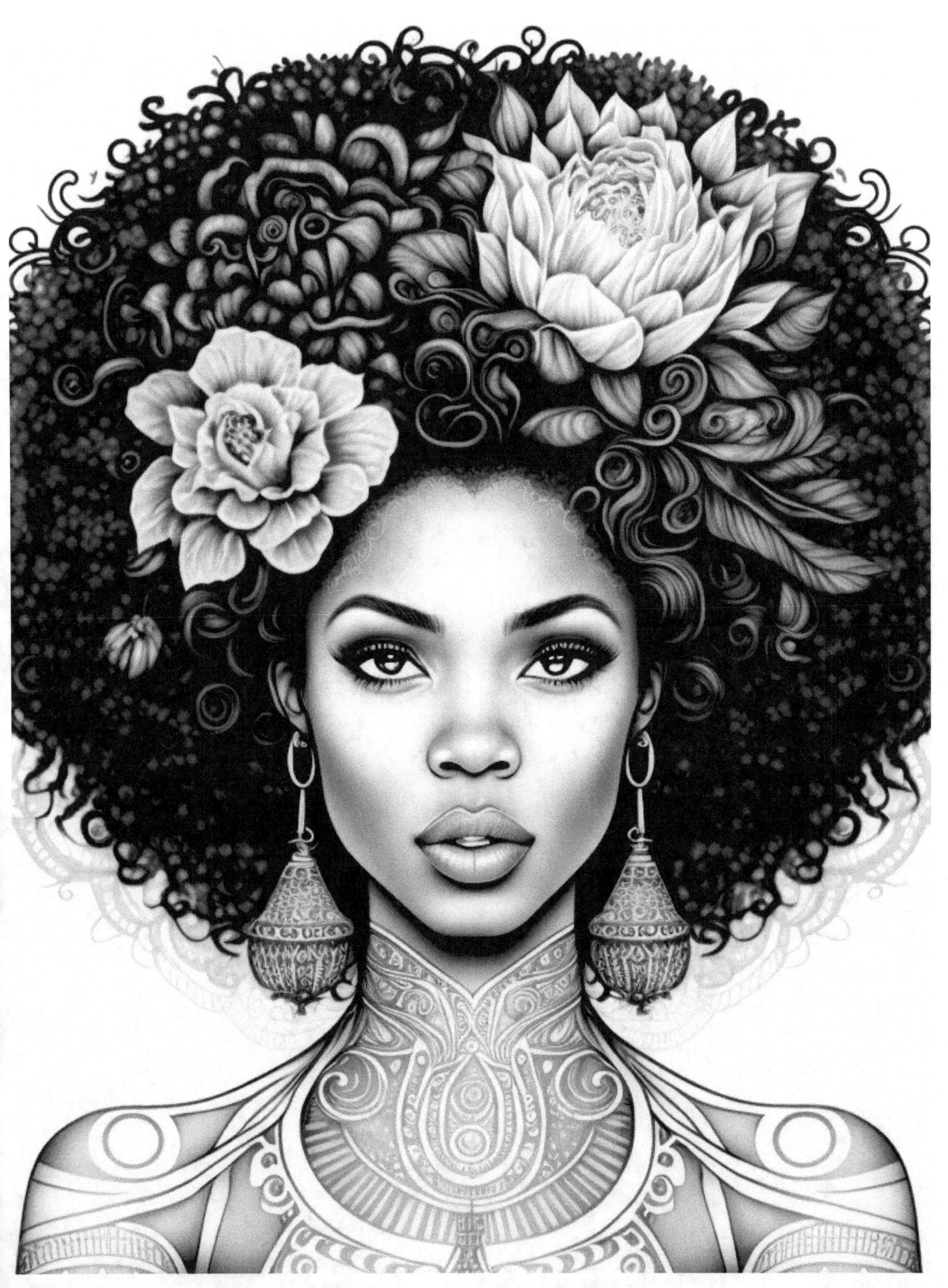

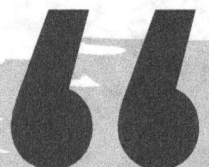

"Have a vision of excellence, a dream of success, and work like hell."

– Dr. Samuel DuBois Cook

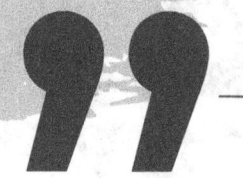

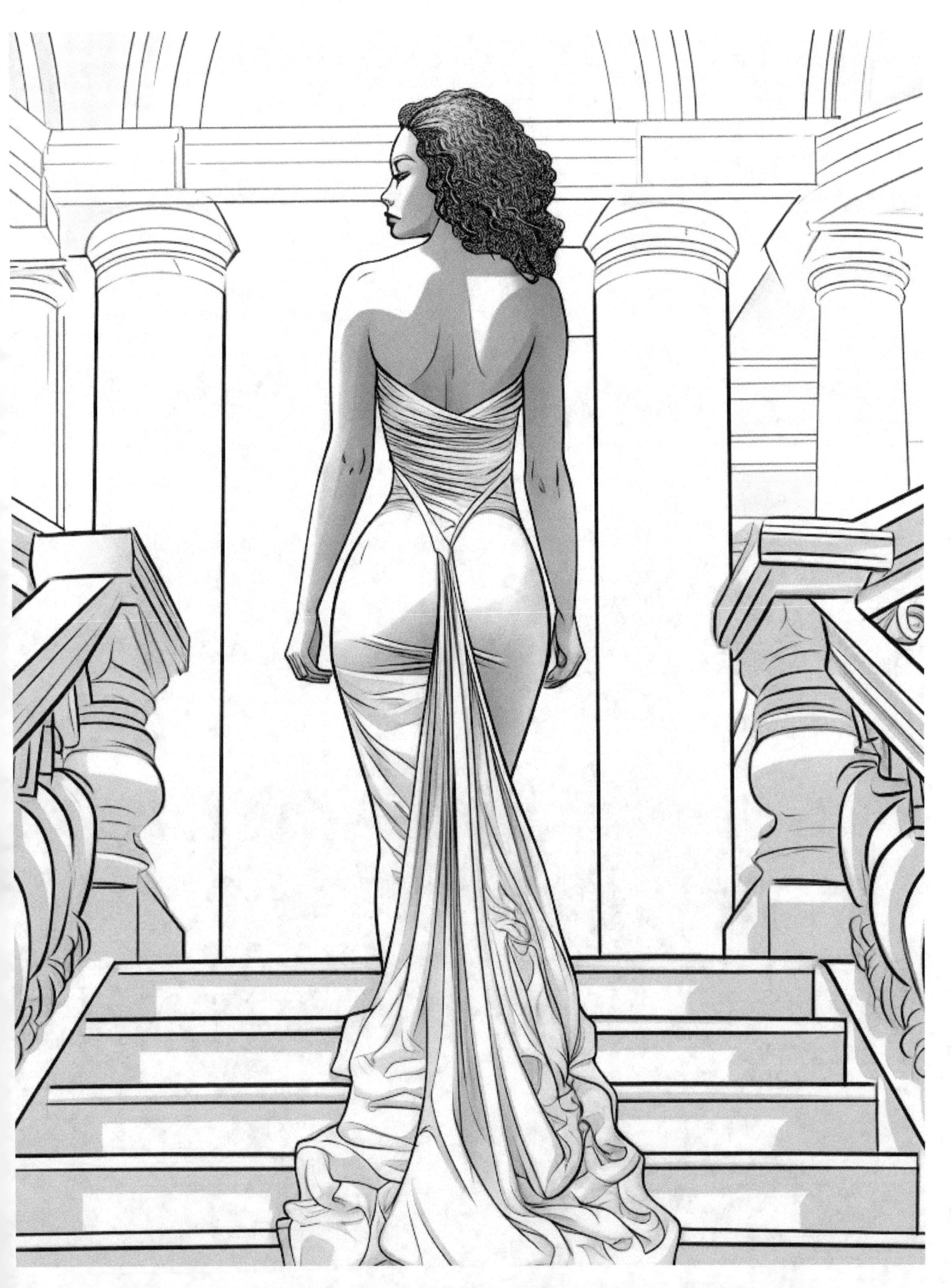

"You have the power to protect your peace."

– unknown

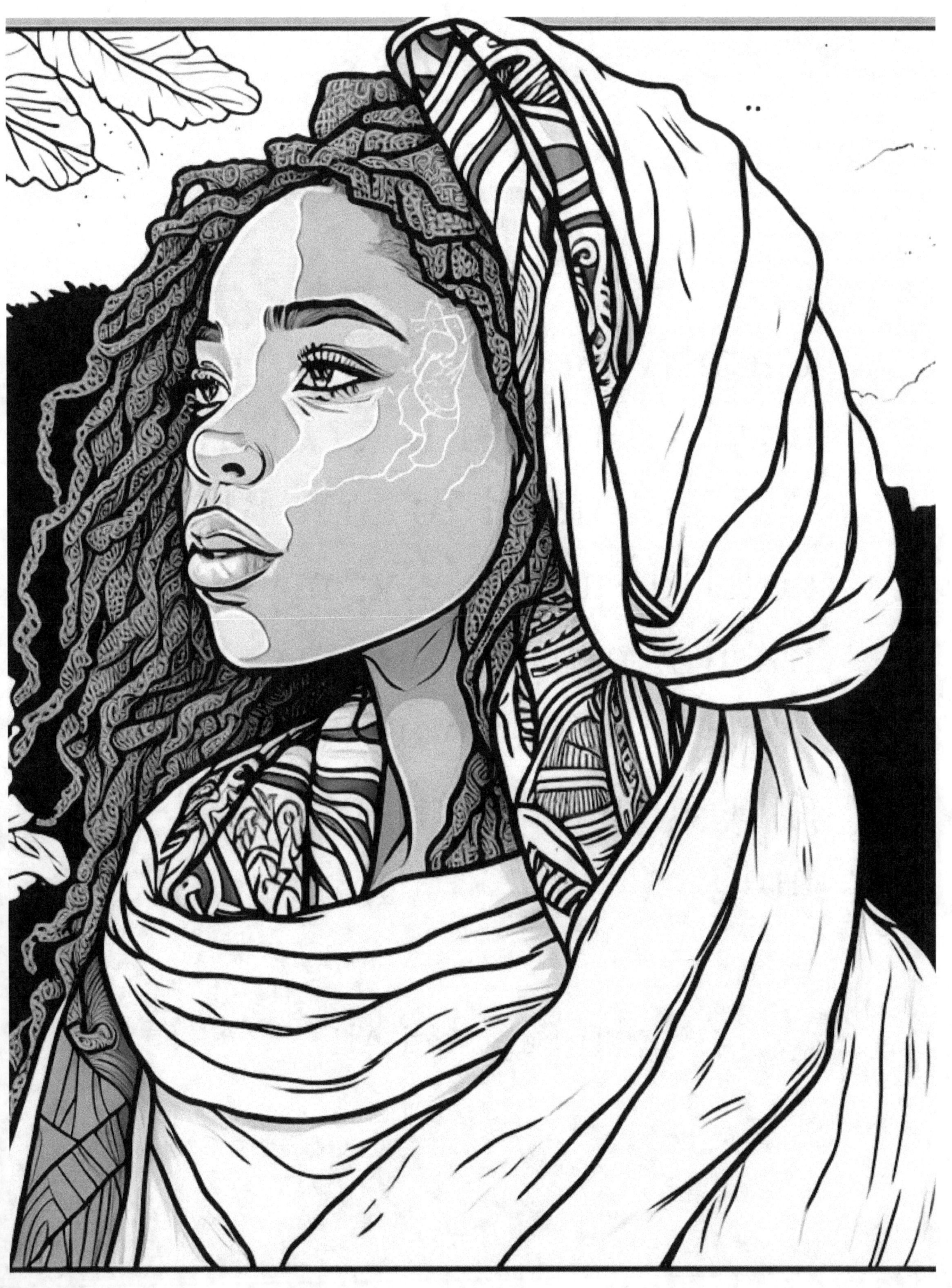

I am America. I am the part you won't recognize. But get used to me. Black, confident, cocky; my name, not yours; my religion, not yours; my goals, my own; get used to me.

- Muhammad Ali

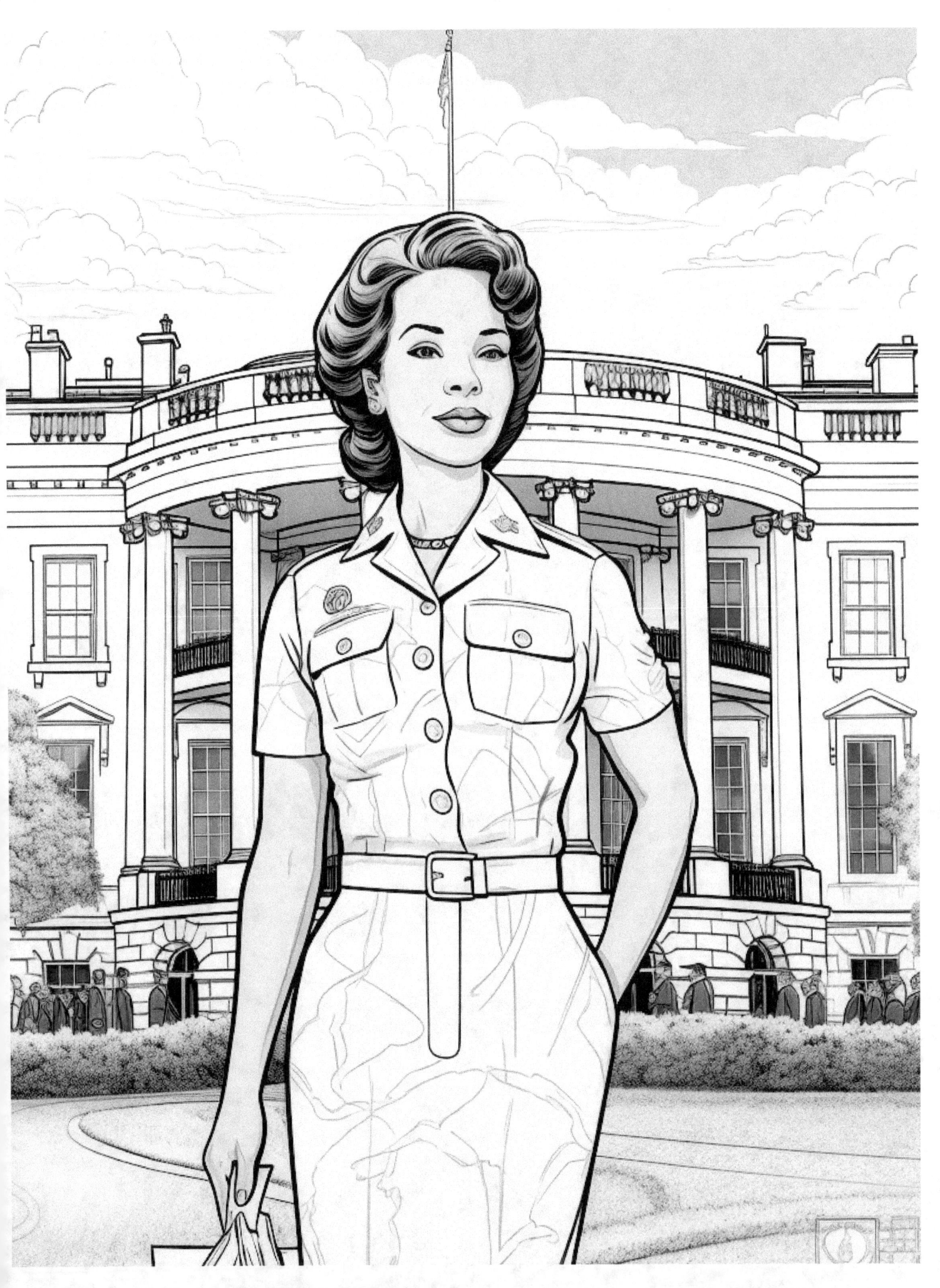

"KEEP MOVING,
the best is yet to come".

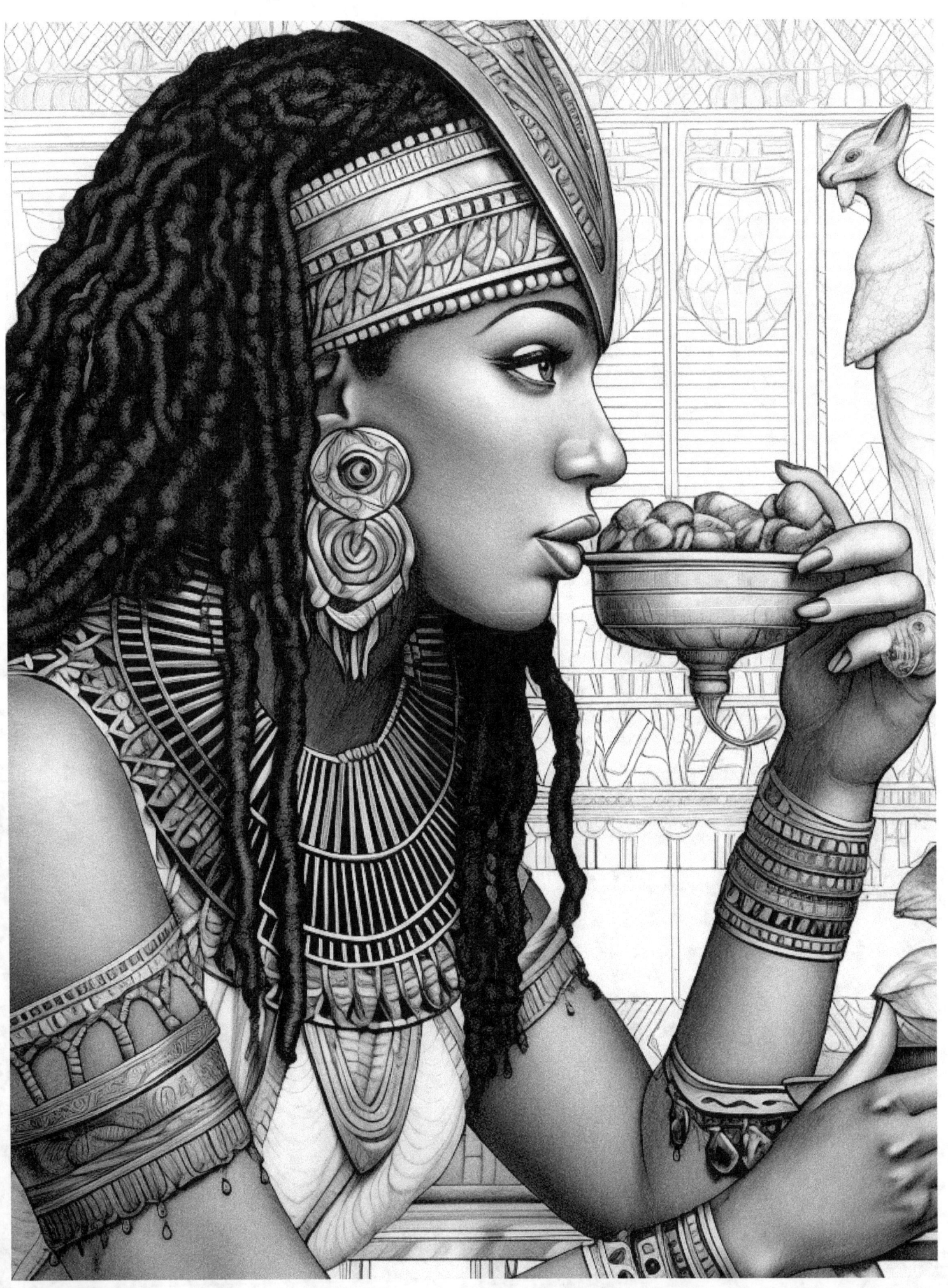

If you have no critics you'll likely have no success.

Malcolm X

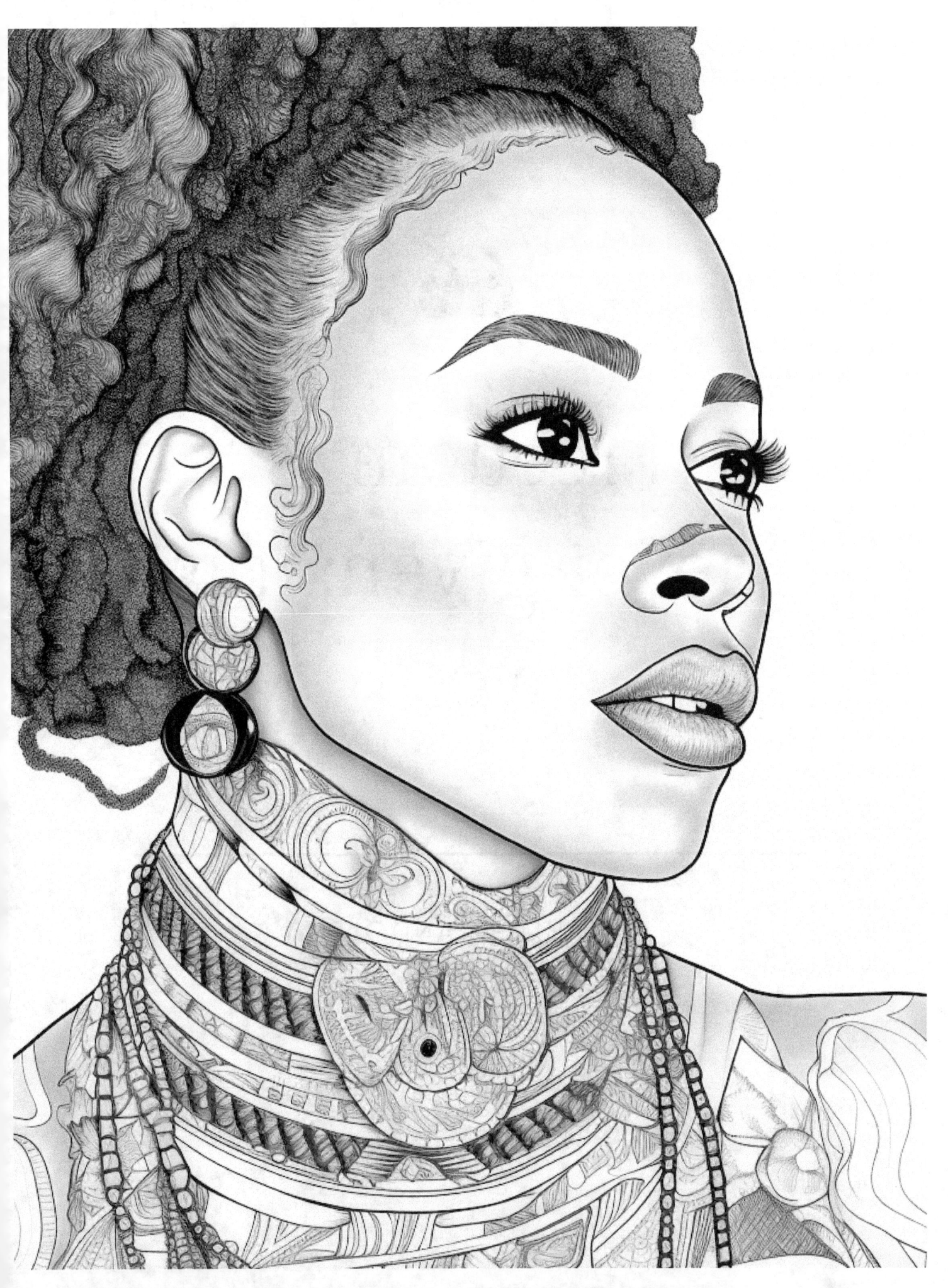

66

Freedom is never given; it is won.

A. PHILIP RANDOLPH

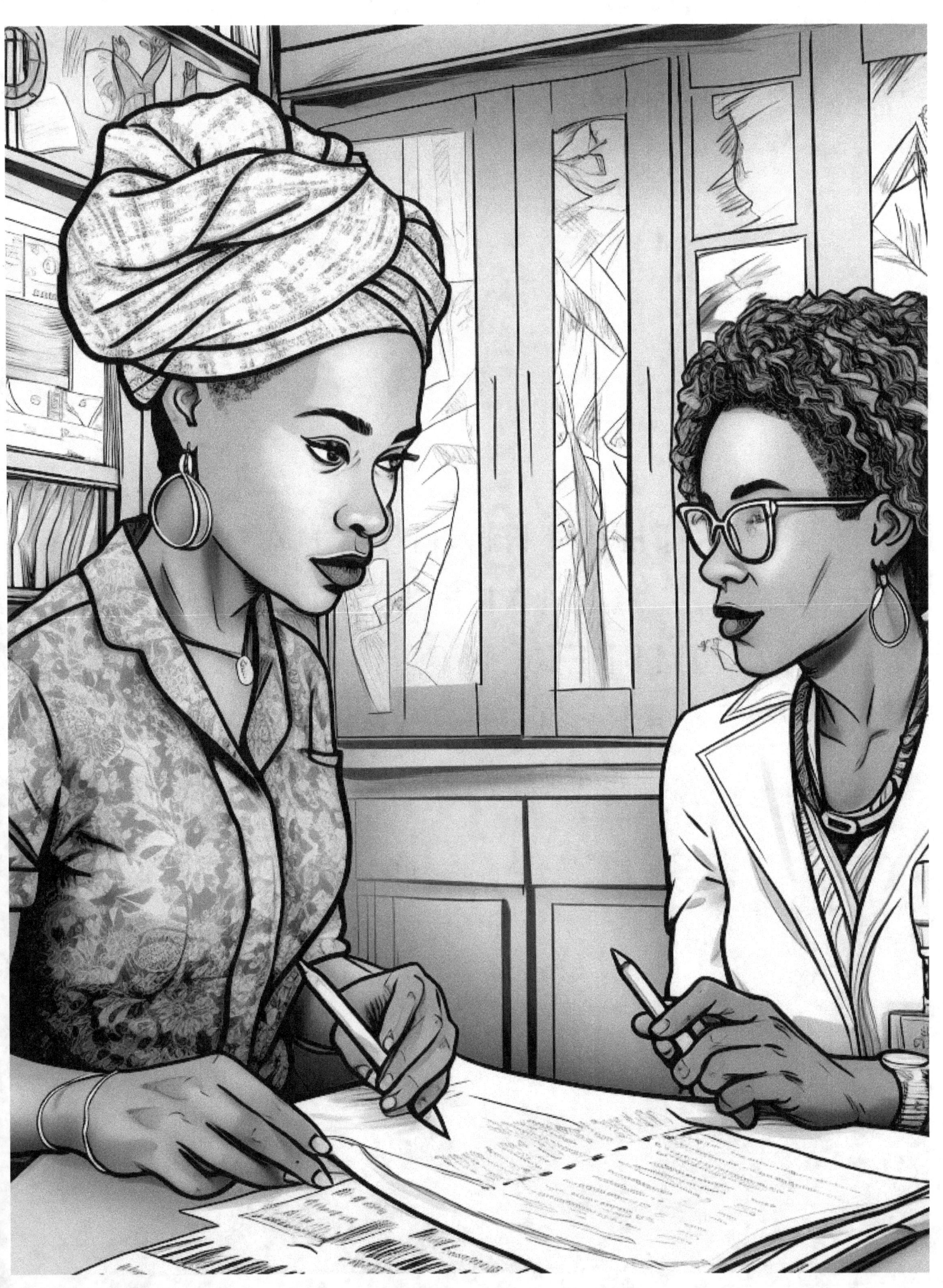

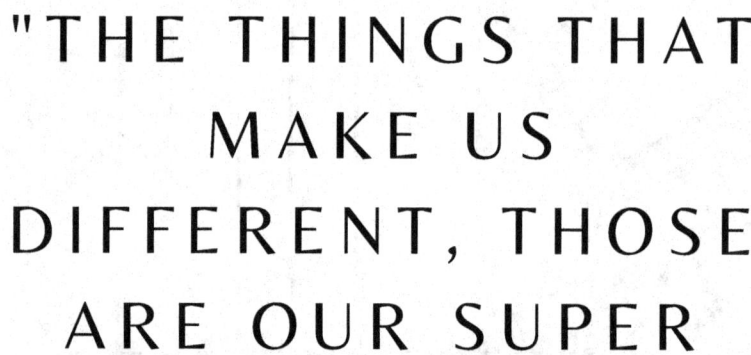

"THE THINGS THAT
MAKE US
DIFFERENT, THOSE
ARE OUR SUPER
POWERS."

LENA WAITHE

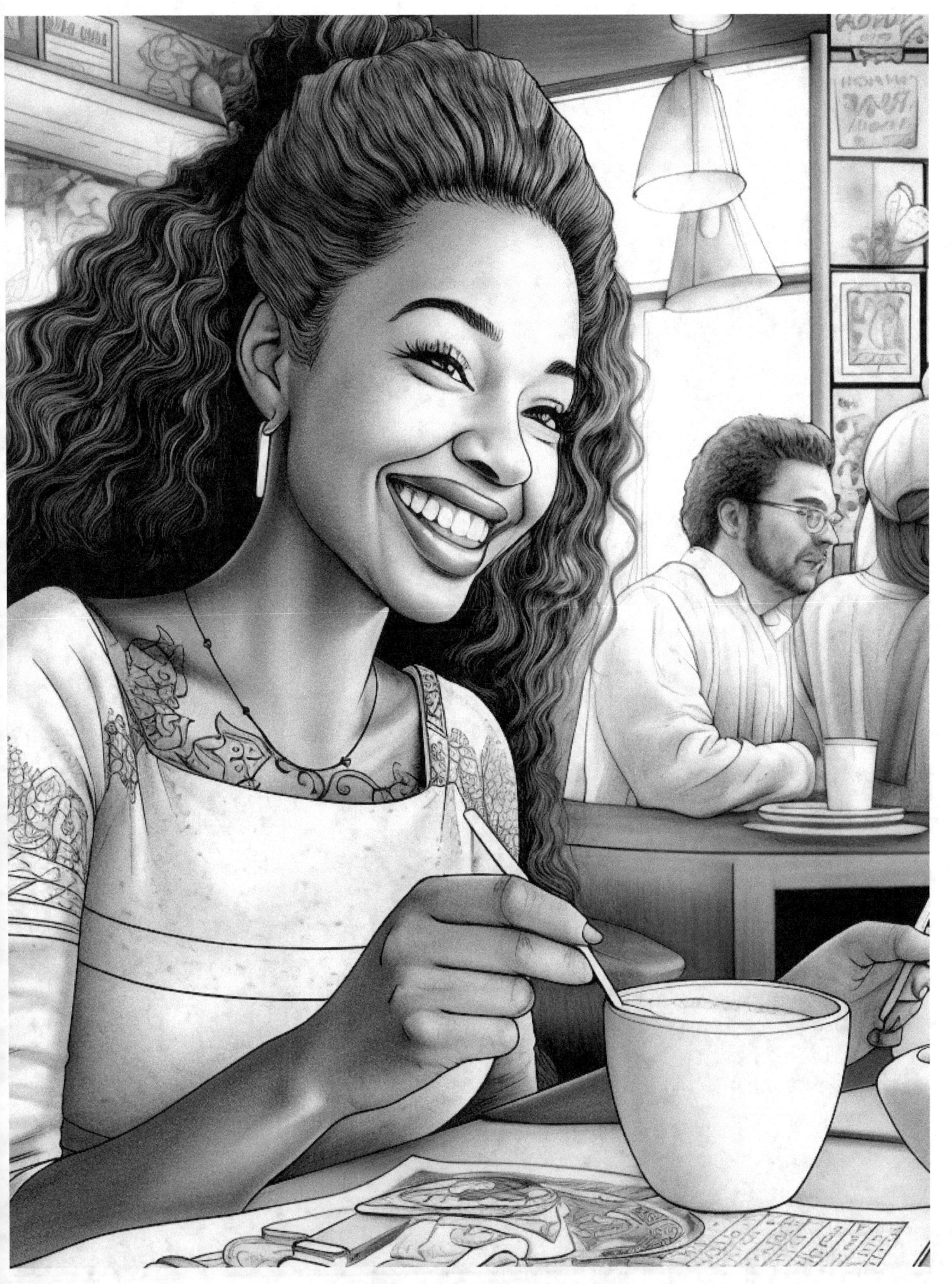

IF YOU CAN DREAM IT YOU CAN DO IT

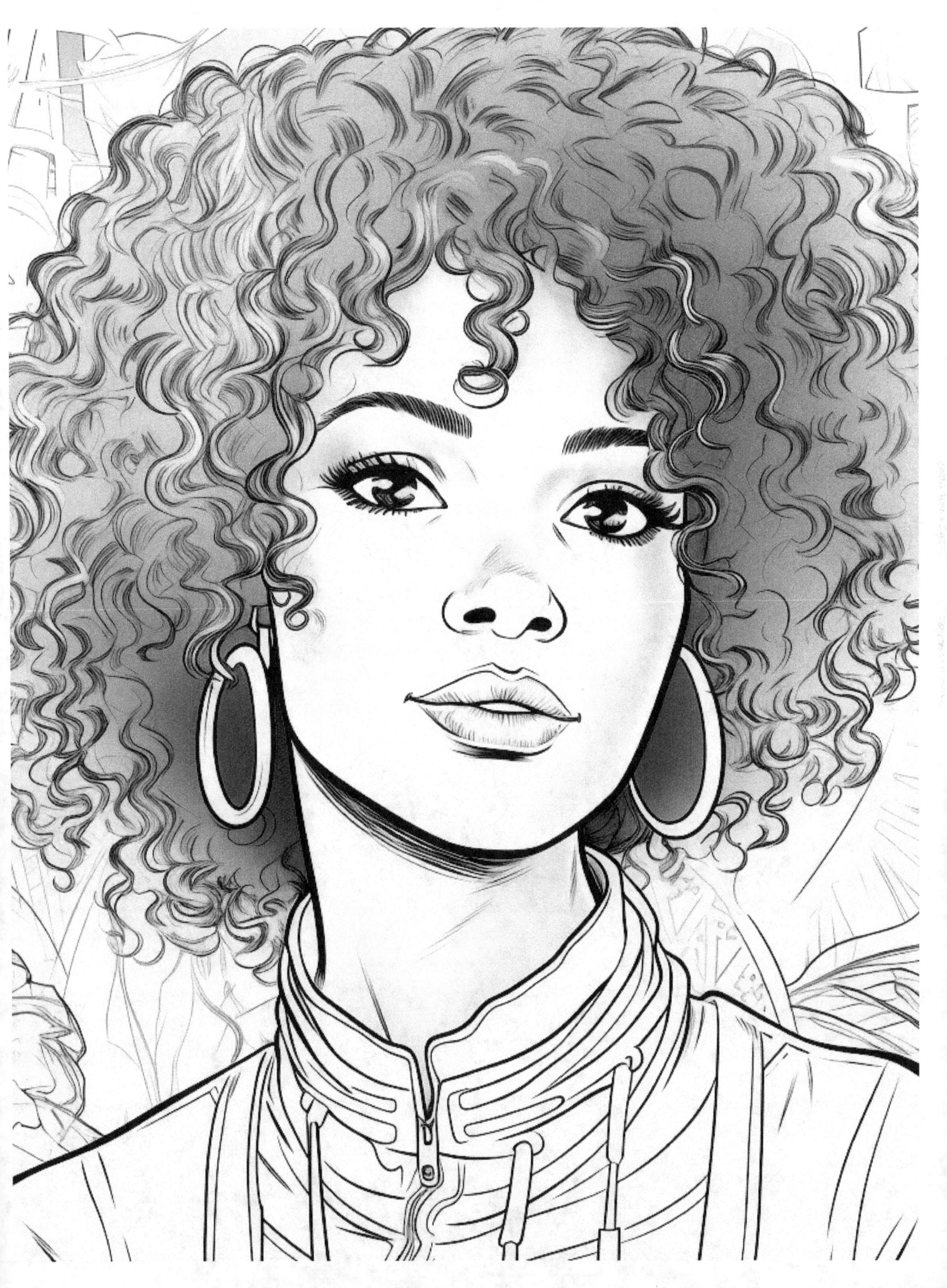

Am I good enough?
Yes I am.

Michelle Obama

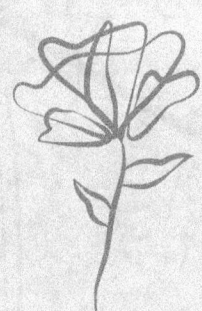

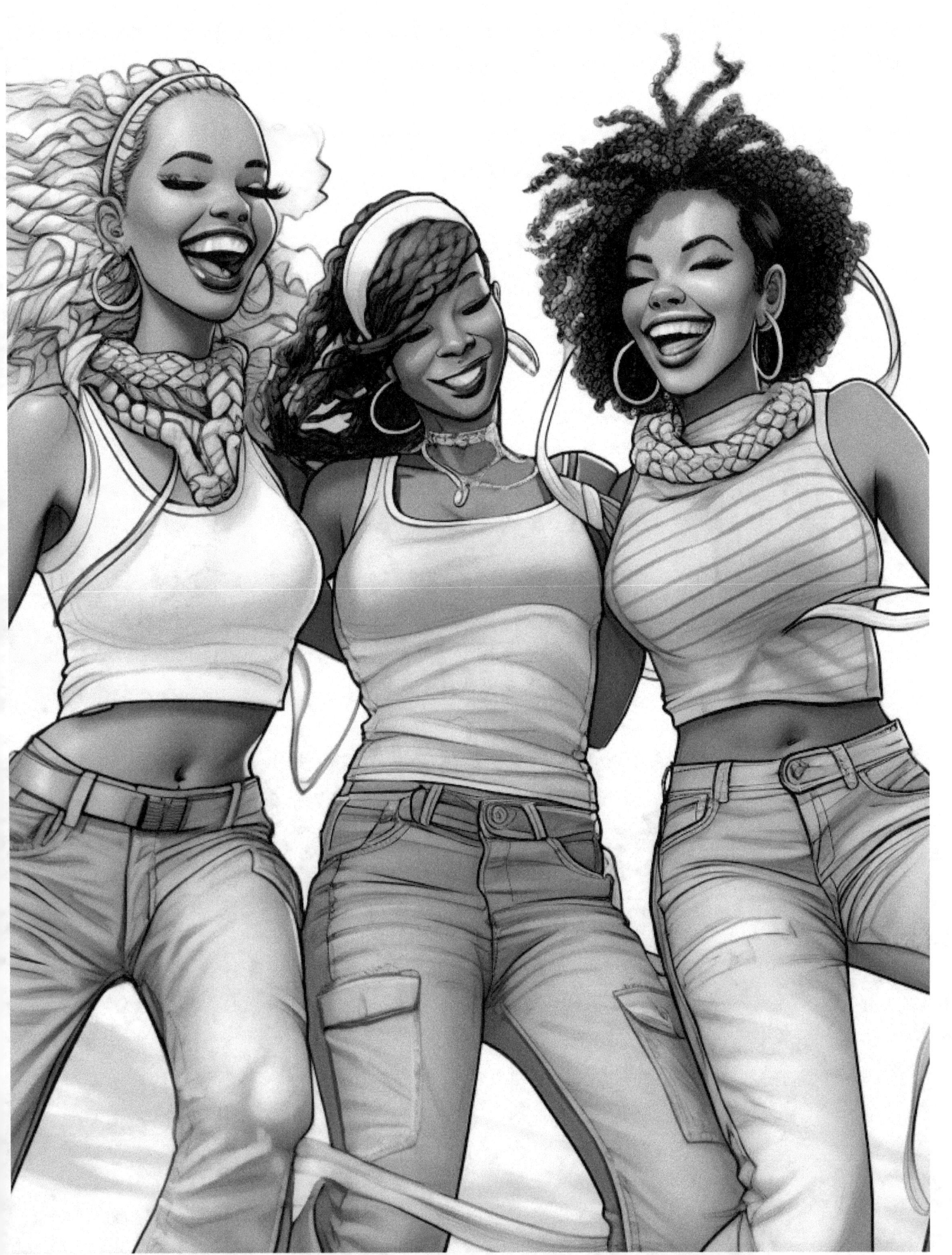

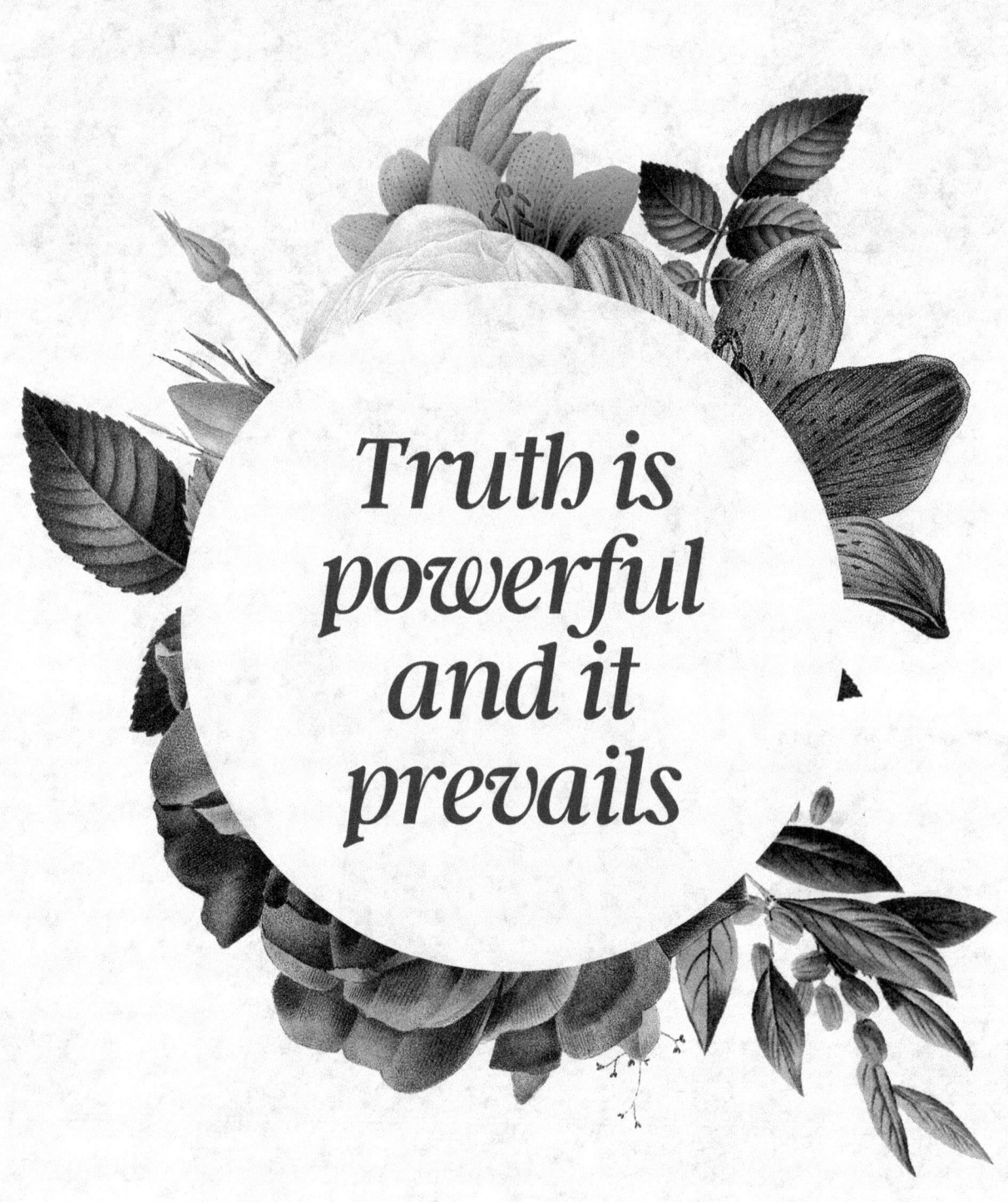

Truth is
powerful
and it
prevails

SOJOURNER TRUTH

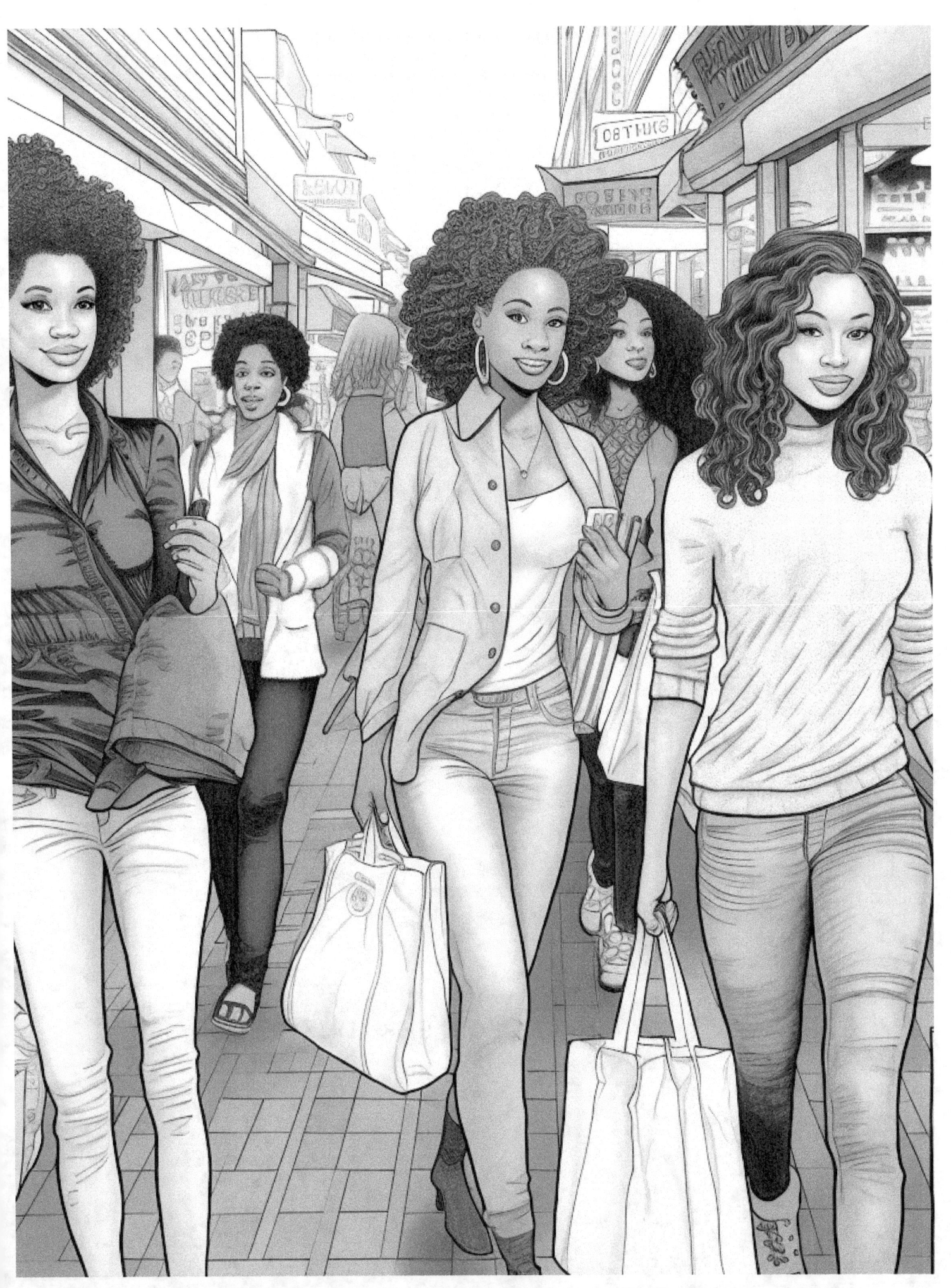

You can fall, but you can rise also.

– ANGELIQUE KIDJO

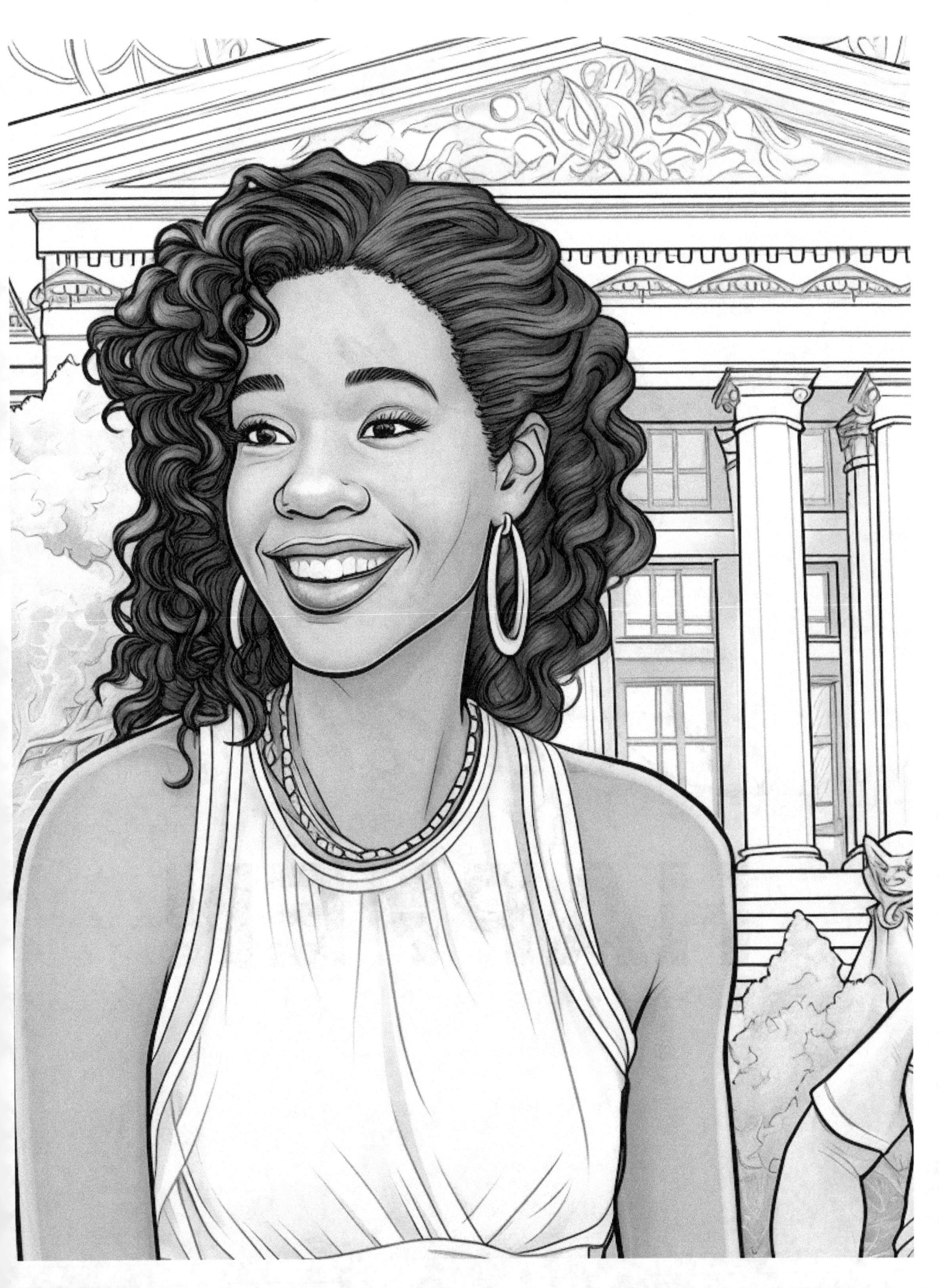

Make YOUR Dreams HAPPEN

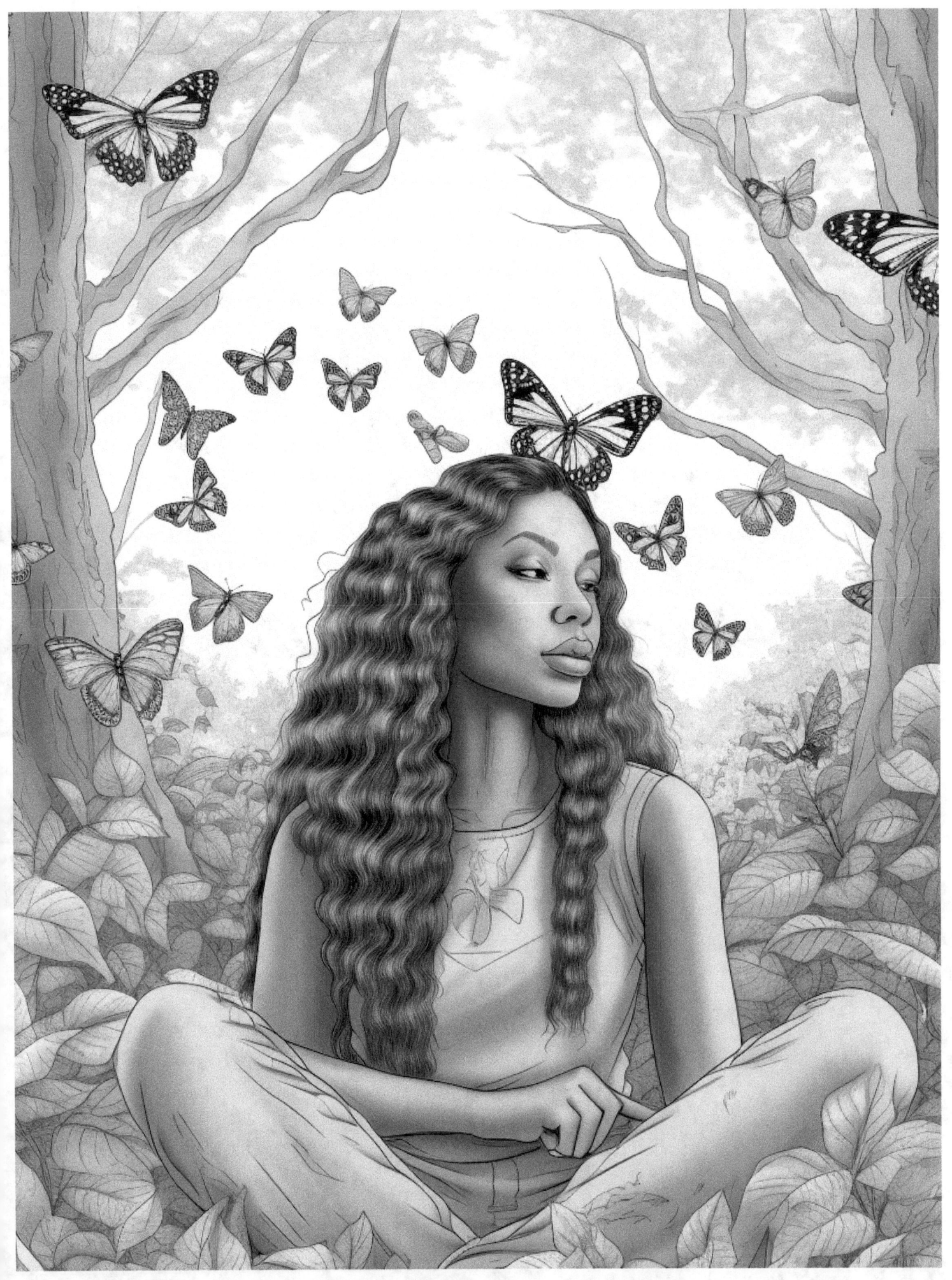

Tell Me Something Good

Chaka Khan

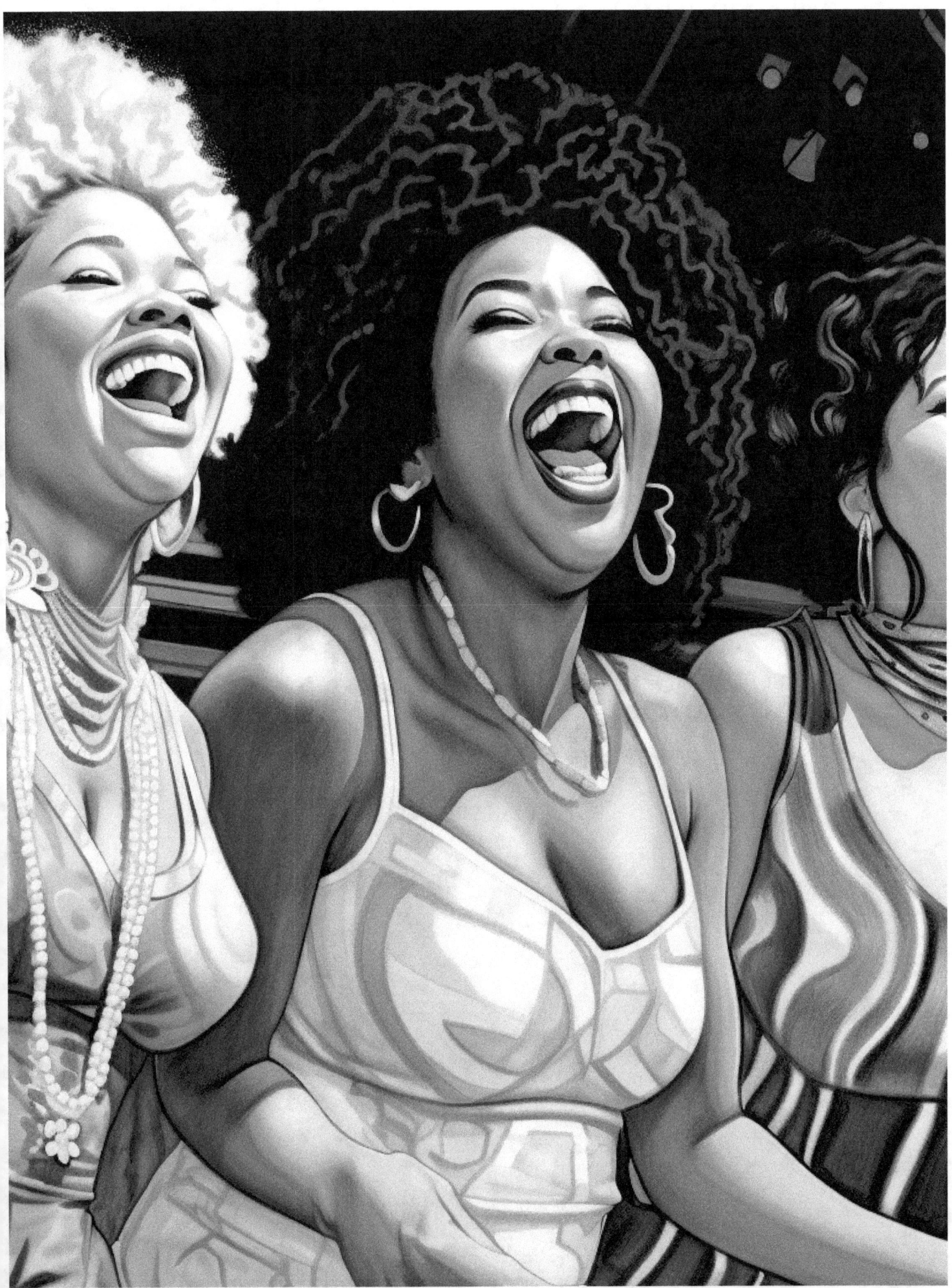

BE BRAVE.
BE AMAZING.
BE WORTHY.

SHONDA RHIMES

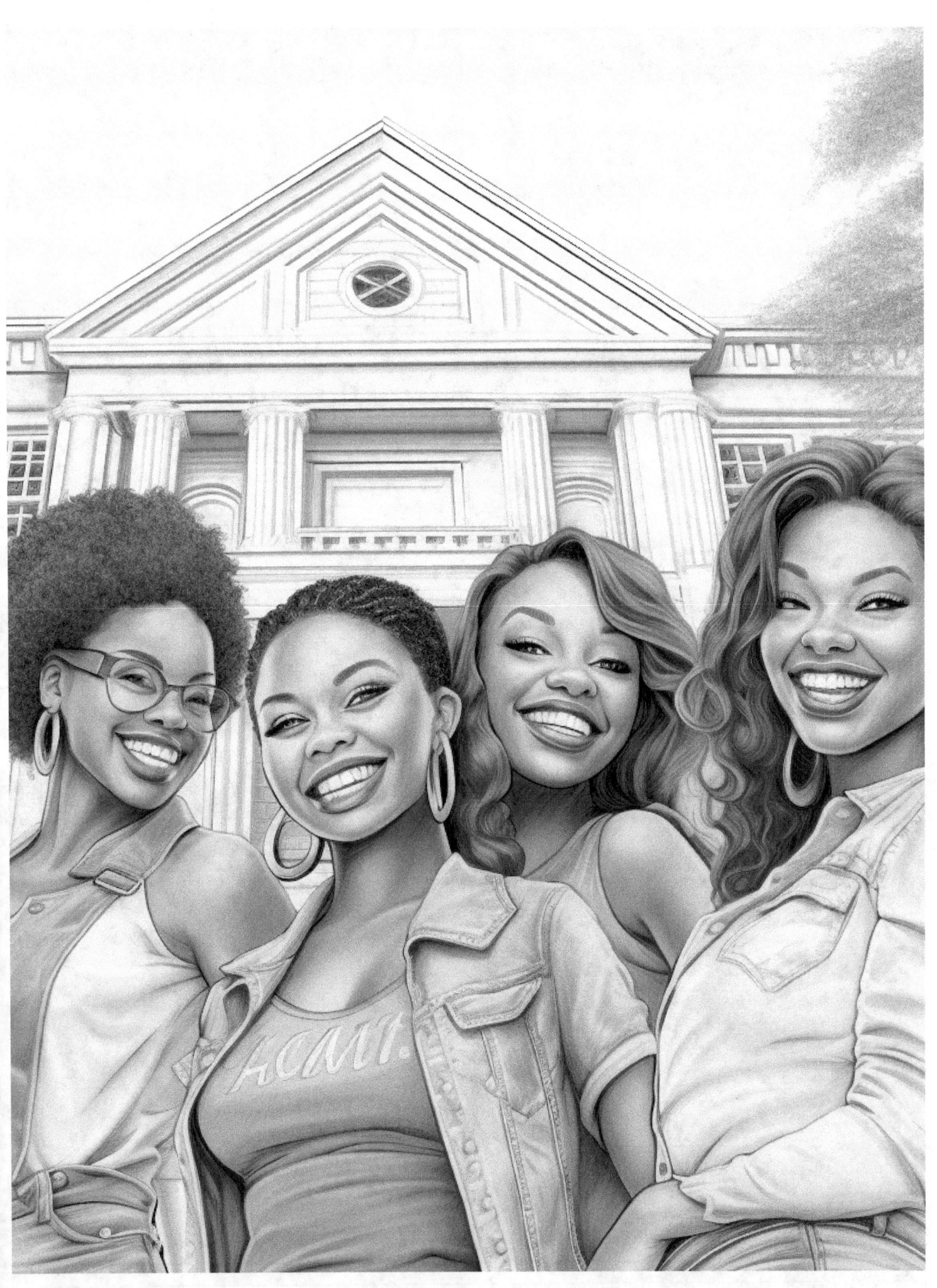

My mission in life is not merely to survive, but to thrive; and to do so with some passion, some compassion, some humor, and some style.

MAYA ANGELOU

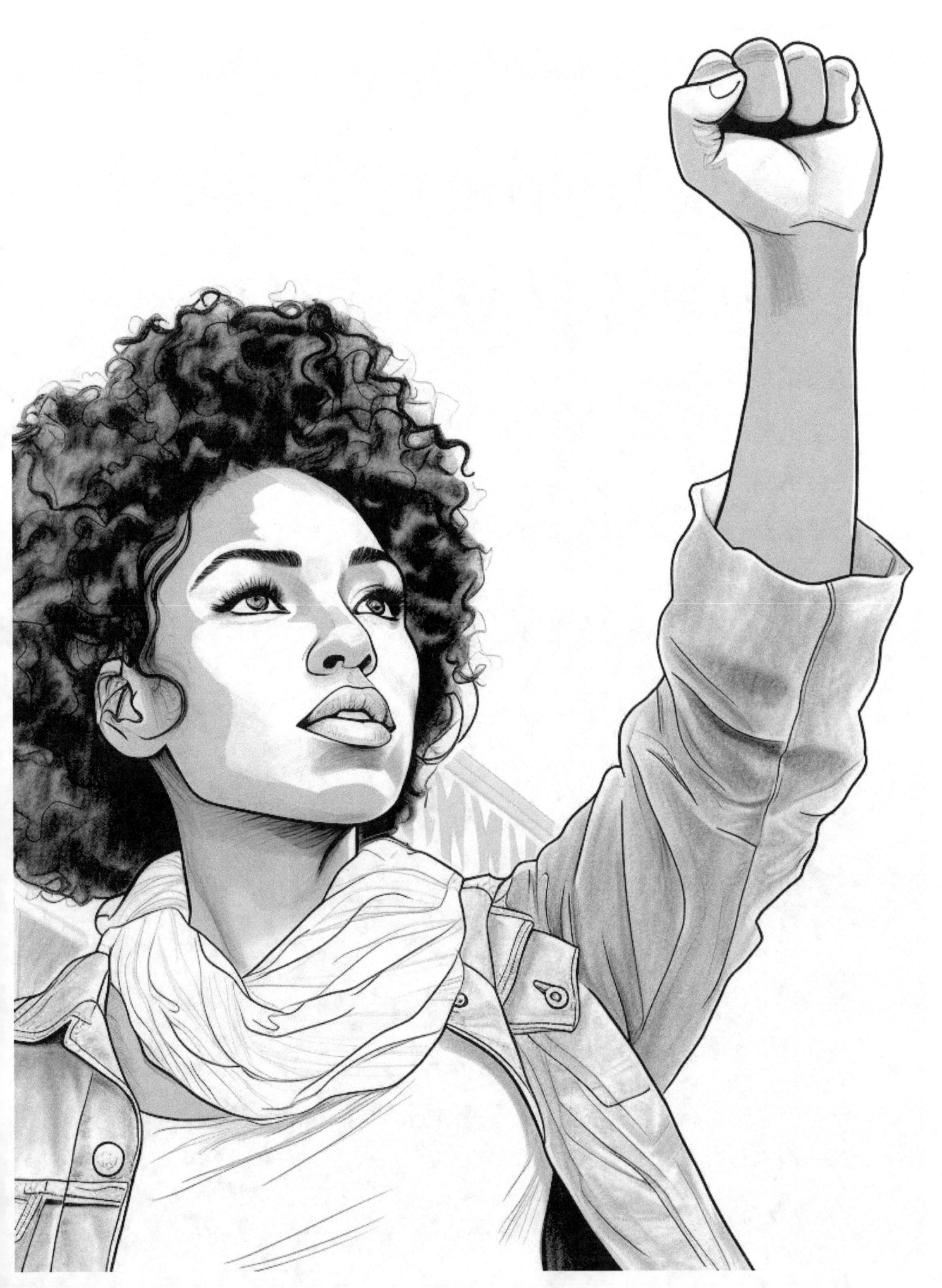

No matter how often you fall from grace, what matters most is how many times you get up.

TARAJI P. HENSON

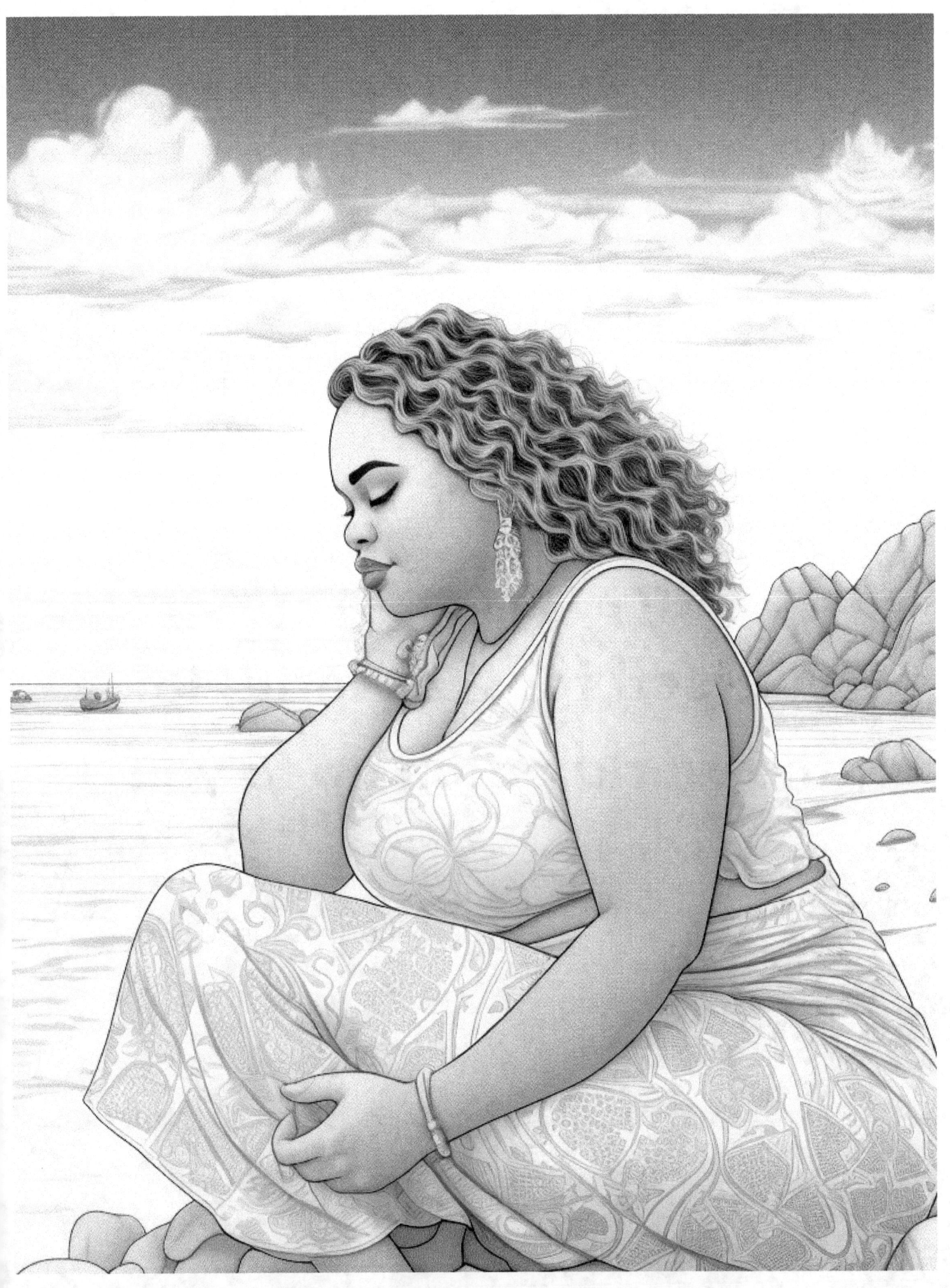

"

Don't try to lessen yourself for the world; let the world catch up to you

Beyonce Knowles- Carter

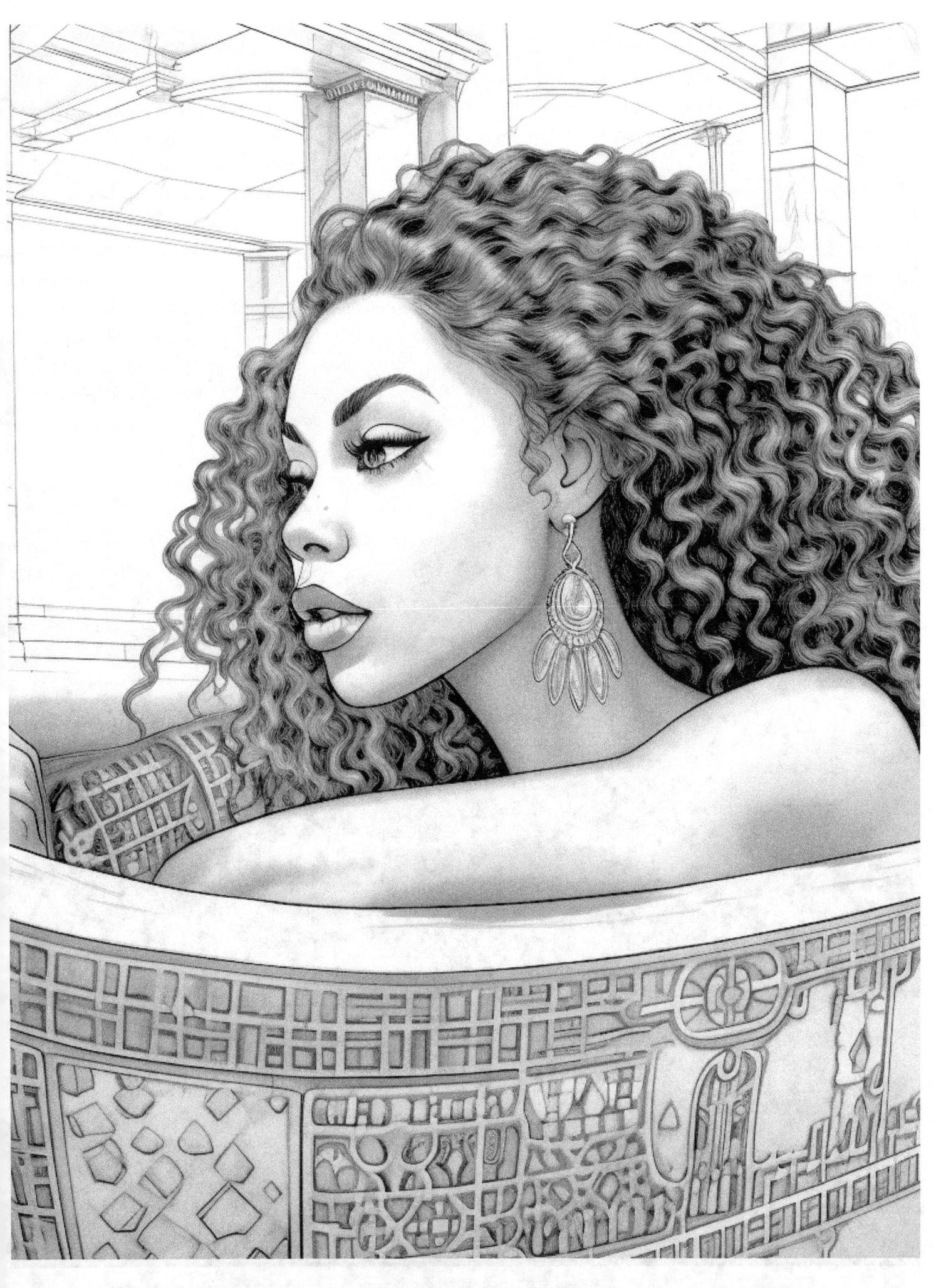

"I'm grateful for all the breaks and honors and opportunities I've had, but I always believe I won't have it made until the humblest black kid in the most remote backwoods of America has it made."

JACKIE ROBINSON

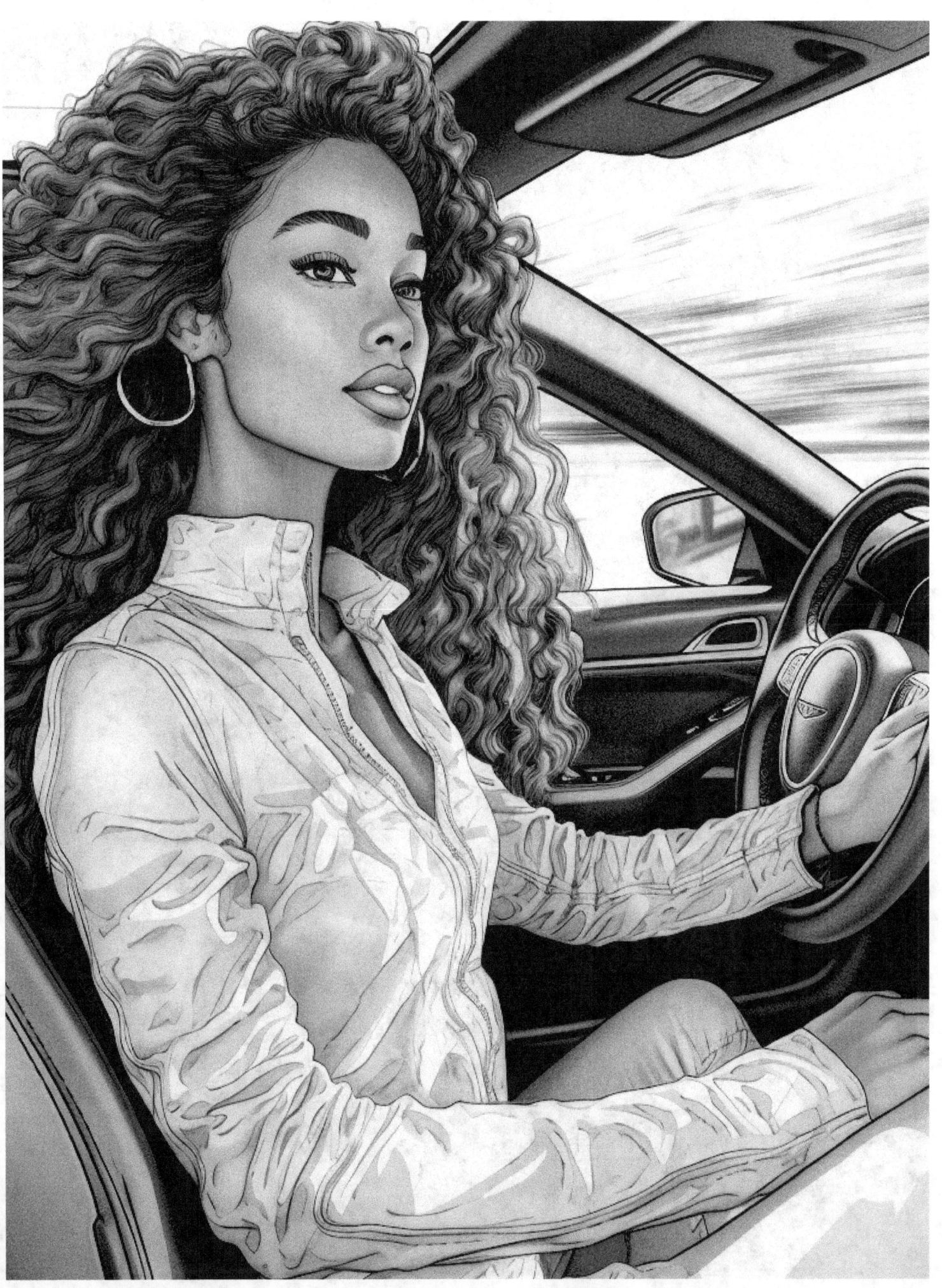

Do MORE of what You love

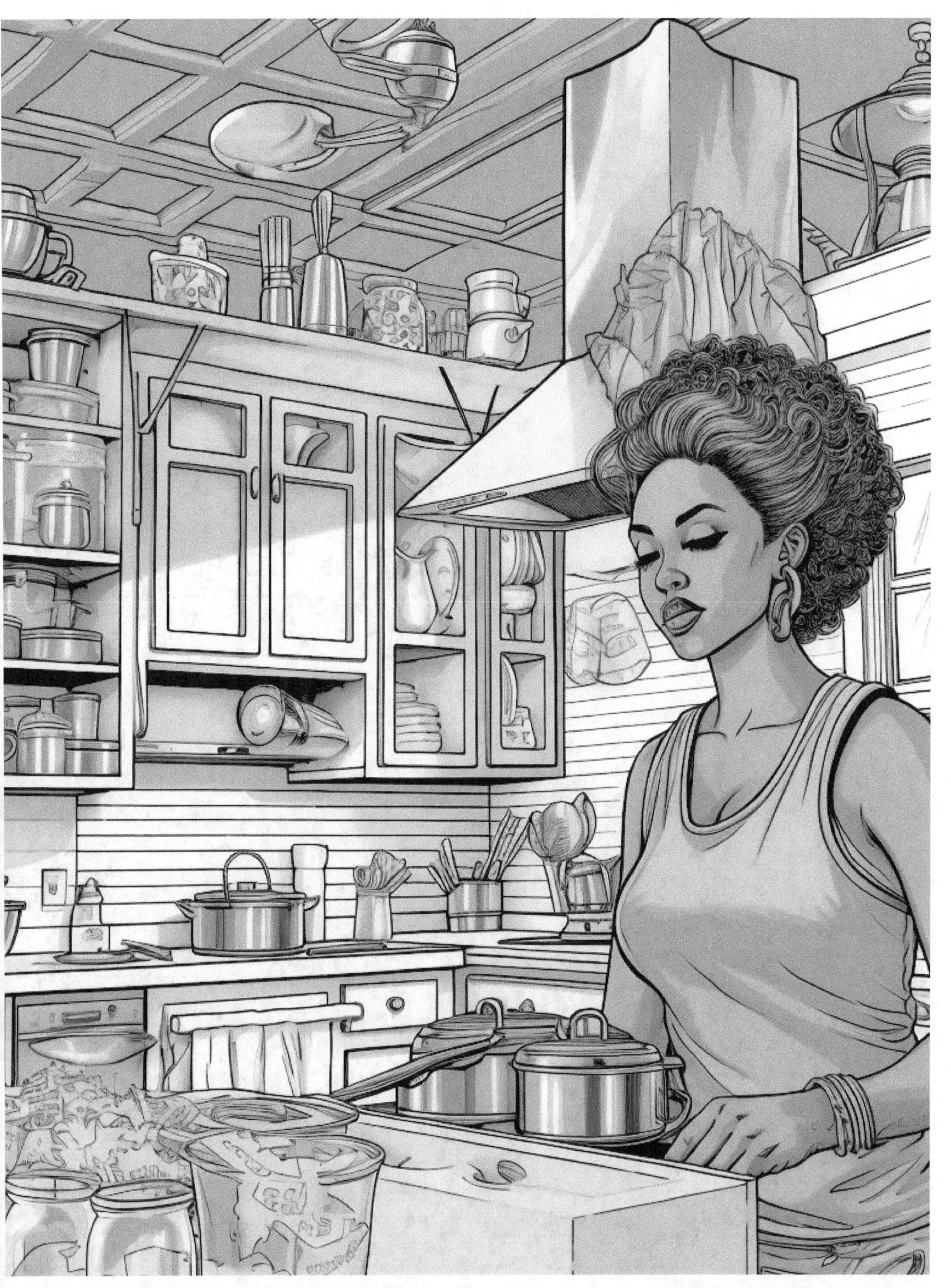

"

_I_ got my start by giving myself a start.

Madame CJ Walker

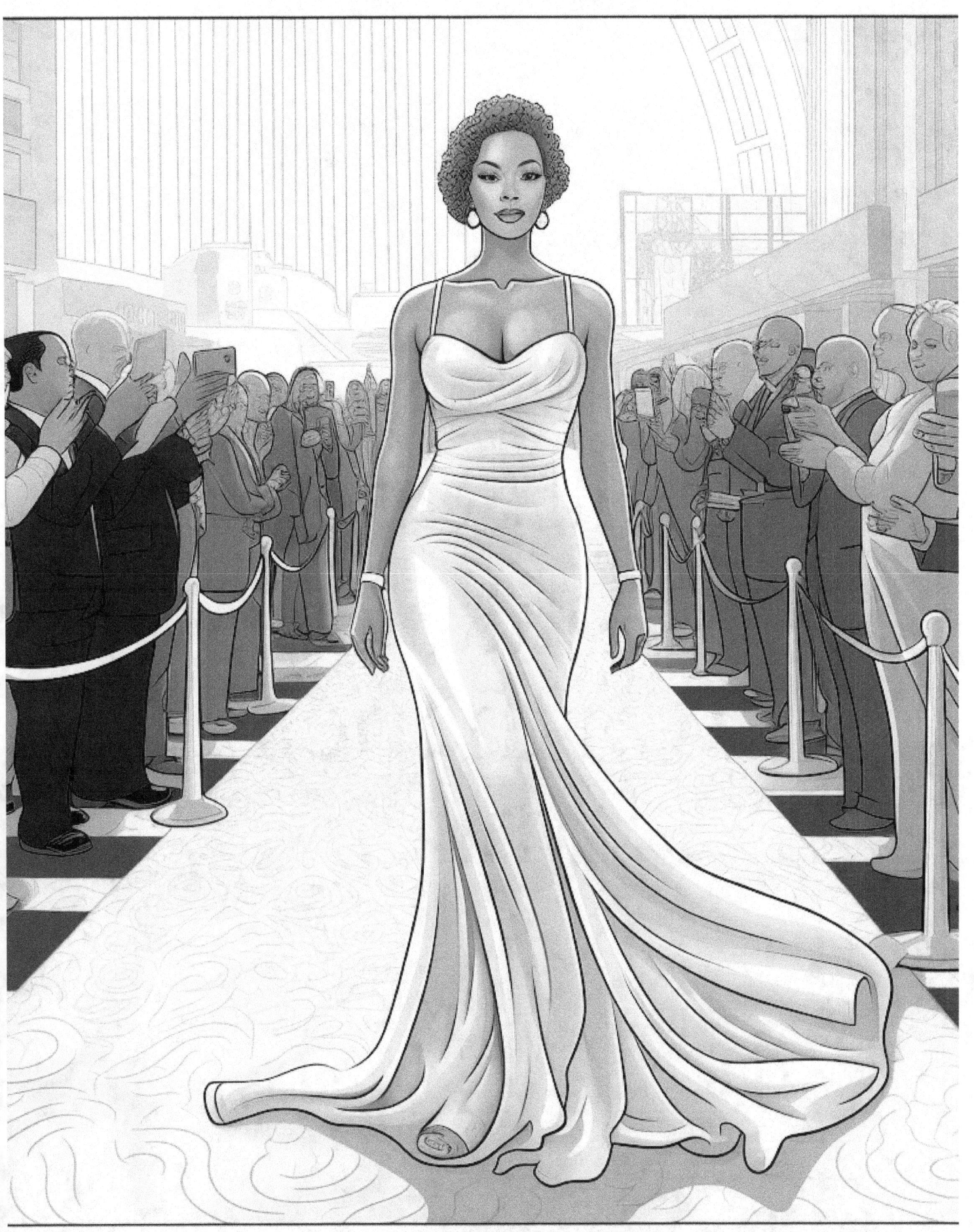

People
will stare,

**Make it
worth their
while.**

HARRY
WINSTON

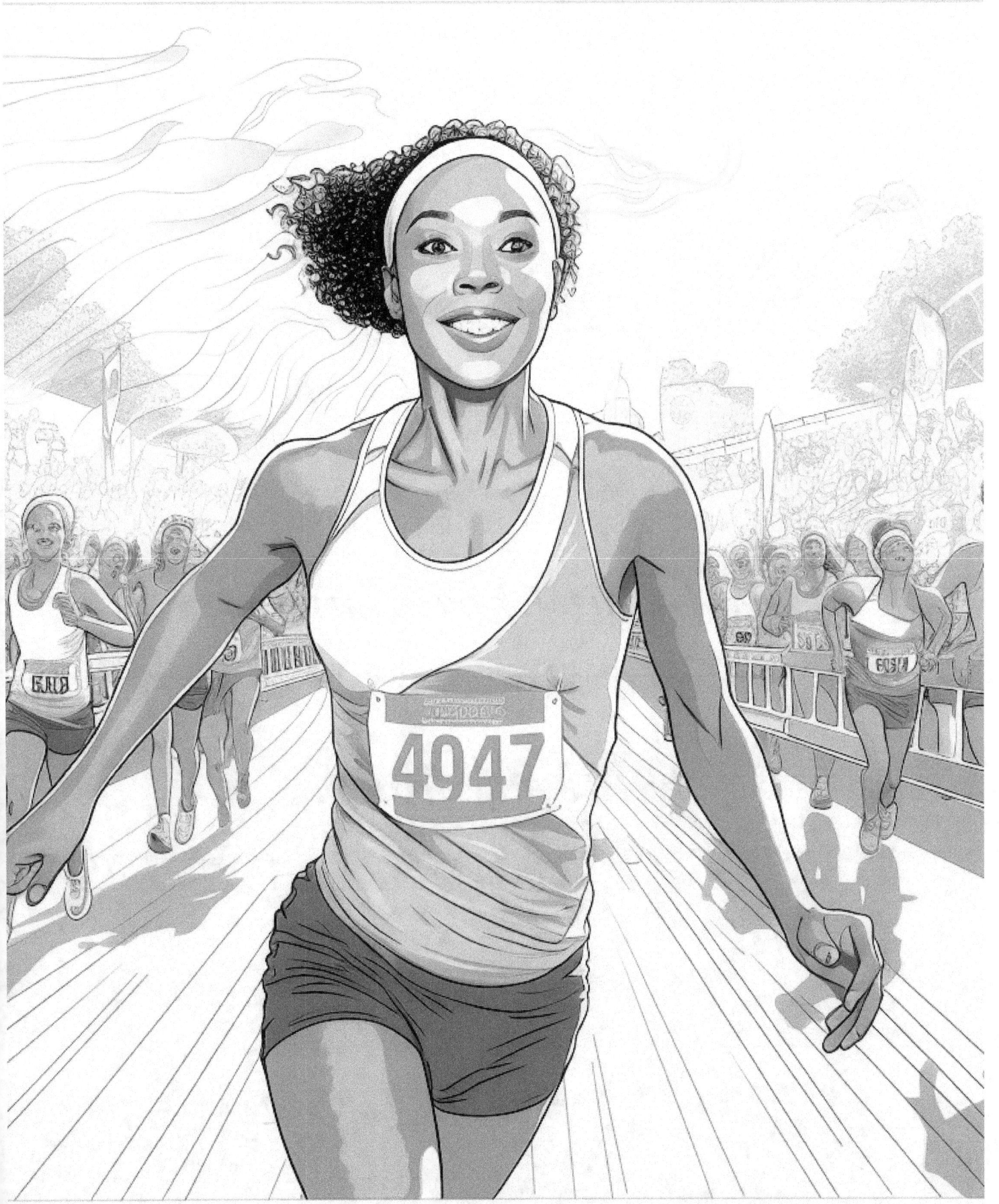

I'm not ashamed of what I am

and that I have curves

and that I'm thick.

I like my body.

- Alicia Keys

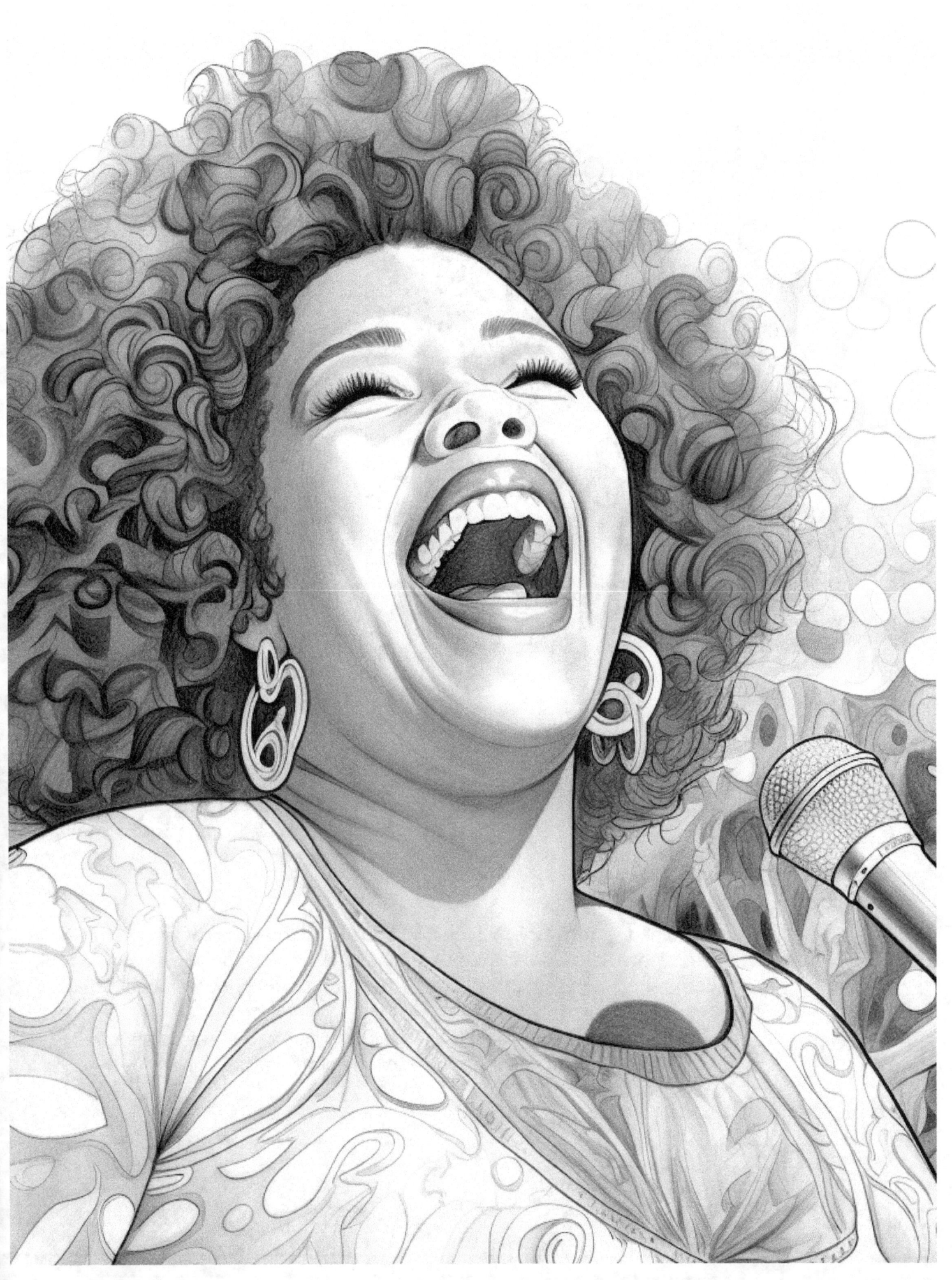

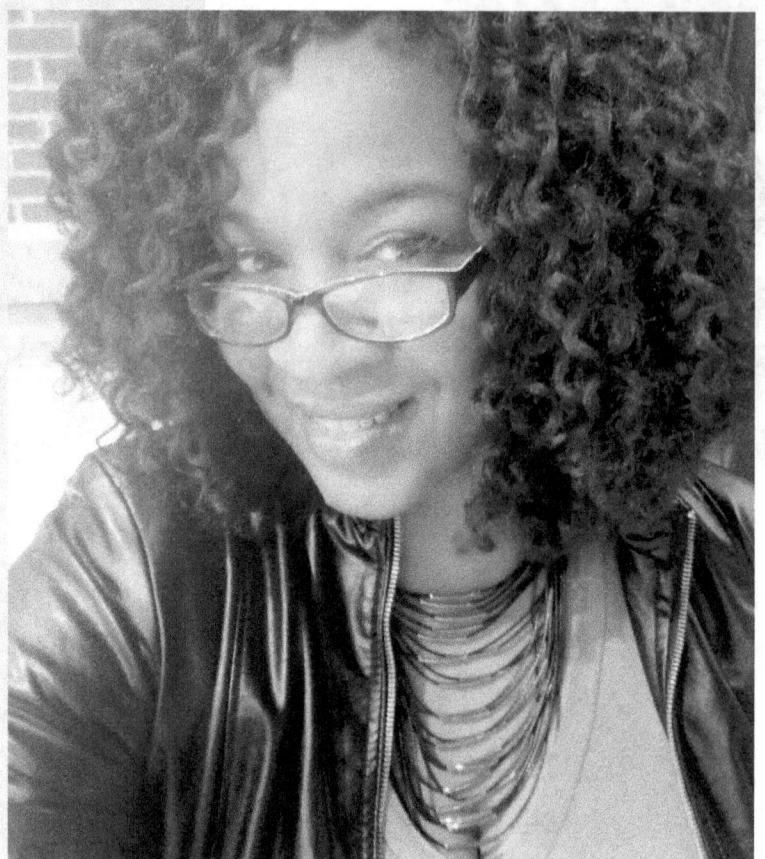

Thank you!

Thank you very much for purchasing my coloring book! It gives me great pleasure to know that you took the time to admire the creativity contained inside its pages. I sincerely hope it has encouraged you in your own artistic pursuits.

If you had a fantastic time coloring and found the book to be a useful and fun experience, I would be grateful if you could post a favorable review. Your nice comments mean a lot to me, and I can't thank you enough for your help.

I'd want to thank you again from the bottom of my heart for selecting my coloring book. I value each and every one of my readers, and I feel blessed to have your support.

Stay in touch!

DEE HAYES

www.TheBlackIsBeauty.com

www.ingramcontent.com/pod-product-compliance
Lightning Source LLC
Chambersburg PA
CBHW080908220526
45466CB00011BA/3508